A teacher's guide to

USING
MEMORIALS

Sallie Purkis

EDUCATION ON SITE

ENGLISH HERITAGE

CONTENTS

English Heritage

UPON 24th JUNE 1978, THE FIFTIETH ANNIVERSARY OF THE FOUNDING OF BRITISH JUNIOR CHAMBER, THIS PLAQUE WAS UNVEILED, TO COMMEMORATE THE FIRST EVER RAILWAY EXCURSION, FROM LEICESTER TO LOUGHBOROUGH, ORGANISED BY MR THOMAS COOK, ON 5th JULY 1841.

PRESENTED BY LOUGHBOROUGH JUNIOR CHAMBER

Mike Corbishley

Leicester City Council
Your freedom & mine cannot be separated
NELSON MANDELA PARK
working for equality

English Heritage

CLOCKWISE FROM TOP: Memorial to a journey, Loughborough station, Leicestershire; aluminium memorial seat for U.S. Army Airforces, Bury St Edmunds, Suffolk; memorial to Nelson Mandela, Leicester; memorial to a Tolpuddle Martyr, Tolpuddle, Dorset; memorial to a painter, Joseph Wright of Derby, Derby; memorial to 17 protestant martyrs of the sixteenth century, Bury St Edmunds, Suffolk; memorial on King Richard's Bridge, Leicester.

THIS BRIDGE WAS ERECTED BY THE CORPORATION OF LEICESTER IN THE MAYORALTY OF SAMUEL VICCARS ESQ: A.D.1862. ON THE SITE OF THE ANCIENT BOW BRIDGE OVER WHICH KING RICHARD III PASSED AT THE HEAD OF HIS ARMY TO THE BATTLE OF BOSWORTH FIELD, AUGUST 22ND 1485. JOSEPH WHETSTONE CHAIRMAN OF THE HIGHWAY COMMITTEE, SAMUEL STONE, TOWNCLERK, E.L. STEPHENS BOROUGH SURVEYOR.

English Heritage

Mike Corbishley

English Heritage

1834 JAMES HAMMETT TOLPUDDLE MARTYR PIONEER OF TRADES UNIONISM CHAMPION OF FREEDOM BORN 11 DECEMBER 1811 DIED 21 NOVEMBER 1891

British Tourist Authority

ABOUT THIS BOOK

This column was erected by a young architect of this town in commemoration of the victorious battle of Waterloo in which British valour was triumphant and secured to the contending powers of Europe tranquillity and peace, June 18th 1815.

Romsey Abbey, Hampshire.

Memorials are mementoes of individuals, groups or events, made retrospectively by the living. There is a long and rich British tradition for commemoration that extends through the private and public spheres, with monuments recording achievement and disaster in the lives of families, the locality and the nation. Most monuments can be found in public areas like streets, parks, churchyards and cemeteries but examples of personal memorials of a more domestic nature come in the form of needlework, pottery, prints and jewellery and have found their way into museum collections.

Memorials are social documents. Family graves provide information about individuals, their family connections, their lifespan - sometimes even their occupations, achievements in life and circumstances of their death. Public memorials celebrate the lives of famous people or record significant events in the history of the locality or the nation. They are all primary historical sources which provide information. Memorials are also a reflection of the opinions and values of the people who erected them.

Memorials are important not only for what they tell us about death but for what they reveal about life at particular moments in the past. They give us clues about taste and fashion, about communal values, about the distribution of wealth and about the status of individuals. They send out messages about the feelings of people who lived before us, emotional responses expressing pride, sorrow, guilt, hope and love. Every memorial, whether a grave in a country churchyard, a war memorial in a town square, a Blue Plaque on a house, a public statue or an obituary in a newspaper can be the beginning of an exciting and original investigation. This book aims to help you and your class

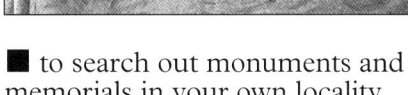

■ to search out monuments and memorials in your own locality

■ to unlock the story behind them

■ to analyse them as historical evidence

■ to make a record of them so that the information they convey will be preserved for later generations.

The studies will raise issues and provoke discussion about the value of having memorials at all, the form they take and the virtues they commemorate - a debate that will become increasingly relevant as we approach the celebration of the Millenium in the year 2000 and the ways in which it will be marked.

CLOCKWISE FROM TOP:
Panels from The Waggoners Memorial, Sledmere, North Yorkshire; War memorial and statue to Queen Victoria, Bradford.

FINDING MEMORIALS

*Potto Brown was born in this village
15 July 1797
Where he spent his life devoting himself to
the best interests of those around him.*

**Street memorial to a local miller, Houghton,
Cambridgeshire.**

There are memorials in every locality, in the street, in the landscape and in museums, as well as the more obvious places like churchyards and cemeteries. Those which dominate public spaces and have influenced the name of the surrounding streets or area will come instantly to mind, but others, which are less famous are equally worth investigating, wherever you live. Use local knowledge from such people as local studies librarians, vicars, long-established residents, pupils at the school and their families.

Coventry Tourism & Conference Office

**Lady Godiva statue in
Coventry.**

The memorials in this section of the book are in a rough chronological order but do not include those in churches, churchyards and cemeteries (see pages 21-26). However, it is necessary to keep a very open mind about date, particularly with memorials in prominent public places. Many were not erected at the time with which they are associated on the inscriptions.

The Victorians and Edwardians were exceptionally keen on rediscovering, interpreting and rewriting English history with a heroic bias. Many public monuments reflect that tradition.

The statue to Alfred of Wessex in Winchester, who died 899 but whose memorial was erected in 1901 is one example. Even postwar new towns and new developments drew on the past when it came to naming streets or erecting statues. There is nothing historic about the Bullring in Birmingham apart from its name and the statue of Lady Godiva who died in 1067 was erected in Coventry in 1949 to provide a historic feel to a newly-developed part of the post-war city.

PREHISTORIC MEMORIALS

It is obvious that in the prehistoric period there were no written or inscribed memorials. However prehistoric monuments do exist.

Although we have evidence of prehistoric burials during the hunting-gathering periods, the main evidence which still survives in Britain, on the landscape and as objects in museums, comes from the first farming period (from about 3500 BC).

The earliest evidence is in the form of monumental tombs. In parts of the country where stone is abundant, the remains will often be in the form of large stone uprights supporting a roof slab. In other places the burial chamber, or chambers, will have been made of wood.

Perhaps the most imposing of the burial monuments is the long barrow. This example (left) is at West Kennet in Wiltshire. It was constructed around 2500 BC. The dead were placed in stone chambers inside an earthen mound, 100 metres long and 3 metres high. Archaeologists found evidence of fifty people buried in this mound over a thousand year period. They think that each body was left to rot away, then the bones were placed in a chamber with pottery and arrows. Then the entrance was sealed up with a great stone.

Round barrows and cemeteries

The word barrow is often used for mounds to cover the remains of the dead, in prehistoric, Roman and Viking times. From about 2000 BC the form of prehistoric burial monuments changed. Round barrows were built, in various forms, often in large cemeteries. After about 1600 BC bodies were no longer buried but cremated and the bones put into pots inside or underneath the barrows.

Discussion points could be

Cost of burial

■ how significant a cost was building a medium-sized long barrow to a community? It has been estimated that between 7,000 and 16,000 construction hours were needed.

Grave goods

■ what sort of things were buried with the dead?

English Heritage/Skyscan Balloon Photography

■ what can grave goods tell us about the dead?

■ or, are they supposed to tell us something about the status of those who arranged the burial?

■ what were the views of other peoples in the past, or today, about objects buried with the dead?

Mike Corbishley

ABOVE & BELOW: Trajan's Column, Rome.

ROMAN MEMORIALS

The Romans were one of the most prolific producers of memorials in the ancient world. One of the most famous Roman memorials is Trajan's Column, put up in AD 113 in Rome. Trajan built it as a memorial to his victory over the Dacians. The section (below) shows soldiers cutting logs and turfs to construct a rampart. In the foreground two ditches are being dug and earth is being removed in baskets.

Although Britain was one of the outer provinces many memorials of different sorts have survived. Most museums with Roman collections will have some inscriptions - religious dedications, tombstones or building inscriptions, for example.

Tombstones

This tombstone (right) is from the first capital of Roman Britain, Camulodunum (Colchester), and is the memorial to a cavalryman attached to the Twentieth Legion.

What can we learn about the Romans and their attitude to the native Britons from this tombstone? The inscription reads

Longinus, son of Sdapezematygus, a duplicarius (junior officer) from the First Thracian Cavalry Squadron, from the district of Sardica (now in Bulgaria), aged 40, served 15 years, lies buried here. His heirs set up this as directed in his will.

The inscription gives much more information than modern tombstones do but the sculpture (above right) is even more instructive. Longinus is shown on horseback wearing scaled armour. Below him is the cowering and naked figure of a Briton. The illustration demonstrates the authority of Rome over the 'barbarian' tribes in conquered provinces.

The tombstone has been mutilated and broken, probably during Queen Boudica's uprising against Roman rule in AD 60.

Also from Colchester is this tombstone (below right) of a centurion in a typical pose. He is wearing armour and carrying in his right hand a stick made of vinewood. It symbolises the centurion's right to flog men under his command.

Colchester Museums

Mansell Collection

Colchester Museums

The inscription, like most others, contains abbreviations and codes

LEG = Legion

H.S.E = Hic Situs Est (He lies buried here)

> = Centurion

You will also come across other abbreviations such as

D.M = Dis Manibus (to the Gods of the Dead)

or first names such as

M = Marcus

C = Gaius

L = Lucius

Record of water supply on Hadrian's Wall.

There are also tombstones of civilians in Roman Britain. This one was found at Corbridge on Hadrian's Wall and shows Regina, the wife of a man called Barathes who was probably a flag bearer in the army. He came from Syria and married Regina, who was a slave from the native tribe of the Catuvellauni. Barathes freed Regina when they were married.

LEFT: Tombstone from Corbridge.

BELOW: Building inscription from Hadrian's Wall.

Building inscriptions

Hadrian's Wall provides a wealth of inscribed evidence for Roman occupation. This inscription (above) from the fort at Chesters records the provision of a water supply (AQVA ADDVCTA) by the Second Cohort of Asturians under the governor Ulpius Marcellus.

In the Wall itself there are a number of stones inscribed with the name of particular companies. This one, (below left) between Harrow's Scar milecastle and Birdoswald fort, records the building of a section of the wall by the century (a unit of about 100 men) of Terentius.

Follow-up

You might want to follow up work on Roman memorials by considering

■ the difference between Roman and modern tombstones

■ how much information should a tombstone contain?

■ what sort of decoration/ inscription is permissable today? See page 33.

■ is there any evidence of abbreviation on memorials today?

SAXON, VIKING AND CELTIC MEMORIALS

Even where inscriptions do not provide personal stories, Celtic, Saxon and Viking crosses and stones provide examples of pattern and decoration and carved religious symbols. You may also think it interesting to analyse the source of stone for these ancient memorials and to think about how they were transported, carved and erected.

RIGHT: An Anglo-Saxon gravemarker from Lindisfarne

The Bewcastle Cross, Cumbria.

Anglo-Saxon

A good example of an Anglo-Saxon memorial is the cross at Bewcastle in Cumbria. This high cross stands next to the church of St Cuthbert. The shaft is 4.4m tall. The head of the cross was recorded during the seventeenth century but has now been lost. The shaft is cut from a single stone with elaborate carving on each of the four faces

■ the west face has carvings of St John the Evangelist, Christ and St John the Baptist

■ the east face has a vine scroll with birds and beasts

■ the narrow north and south faces are panels with vine scrolls, interlacing patterns, chequerwork and a sun dial.

The date of the Bewcastle cross is thought to be late seventh to early eighth century AD. The evidence is from the style of the carving but

also from eight lines of runes (below the figure of Christ) thought to commemorate Alcfrith, son of Oswiu who ruled between 641 and 670.

Viking

The first recorded Viking raid on England was in AD 793. The event was listed in the Anglo-Saxon Chronicle. Part of the legacy of the Vikings in Britain was their sculpture and inscriptions. In some parts of the country you will find Viking sculpture in museums. Look out for decorated gravemarkers.

You could follow-up Anglo-Saxon and Viking memorials by extension work into

■ styles of decoration (see video page 35)

■ documentary evidence

This Anglo-Saxon gravemarker from Lindisfarne (above) shows warriors on one face, and on the other the sun and the moon. These warriors may be Viking raiders, but it is possible they may represent Domesday. If they are Vikings then there are a number of documents which you can use as further evidence

We and our fathers have lived in this fair land for nearly three hundred and fifty years, and never before has such an atrocity been seen in Britain as we have now suffered at the hands of a pagan people.
Alcuin, a scolar and teacher, writing to Ethelred, the king of Northumbria in the same year. (pagan = Viking)

RIGHT: War memorial in the form of a Celtic cross at Tadcaster, North Yorkshire.

The ravaging of the heathens destroyed God's church at Lindisfarne, with much plunder and slaughter.
Anglo-Saxon Chronicle AD 793. (heathens = Vikings)

Celtic

Most Celtic tribes were conquered by the Romans but two areas remained clear of their rule - Ireland, where the Scots or Scotti lived and the north of Scotland, where the people were the Picts. The Irish Celts raided the Roman-held land and founded settlements in Wales and in Scotland. It was the Irish who brought Christianity back to Britain in AD 563.

In the Celtic parts of Britain stone crosses were erected. They usually have a tapering shaft topped with a cross and circle. This style of decorated cross was a popular grave memorial in the nineteenth century and was often used for war memorials.

Eleanor Cross at Geddington, Northamptonshire.

The Duke of Wellington, Hyde Park Corner, London.

Nelson's Column, Trafalgar Square, London.

ELEANOR CROSSES

Probably the earliest English public memorials are the Eleanor crosses, ordered by King Edward I to mark the places where the funeral cortege of his wife Queen Eleanor, who died on 28 November 1290 at Harby near Lincoln, rested on its way to Westminster.

The king commissioned the crosses from his master mason, Richard Crundale. They are in the form of angled spires, in the early English decorated style. Built in three storeys, a row of canopied gables protects niches where statues of Eleanor were placed - the work of the sculptor William of Ireland.

Only three crosses survive, two in Northamptonshire and one in Hertfordshire. The others at Lincoln, Grantham, Stamford, Stony Stratford, Woburn, Dunstable, St Albans and Cheapside have disappeared. The cross at Charing Cross is a nineteenth century imitation by the architect E M Barry. The Victorians admired the Eleanor Crosses and adopted the form for a number of public memorials including the Albert Memorial in South Kensington and the Martyrs Memorial in Oxford.

STATUES

Statues in public spaces commemorate both people and events. Like the tombs of the wealthy in the eighteenth century, many were designed by popular fashionable sculptors of their day. Many were designed to occupy specific spaces in the cities that followed the industrial revolution. You will find many fine portraits in stone providing opportunities for pupils to study

■ dress

■ body language

■ objects

■ symbols associated with the person commemorated.

Look out for design features, such as

■ steps

■ plinths

■ horses

■ lions.

Often made to be seen from all angles, statues of people are good subjects for practising photogra-

RIGHT: Florence Nightingale, Derby.

phy, particularly in those examples where the designer wanted to create the impression that the subject towered over the more ordinary mortals who would view it from below. Height is a feature of many monuments in public places. The extreme expression of the symbolism of height was in the use of the obelisk as in Nelsons column in Trafalgar Square and the Grey monument in Newcastle-on-Tyne, erected in honour of the Prime Minister responsible for the first Reform Bill. It is also interesting to read that the original design for the monument to the Great

Peter Stone

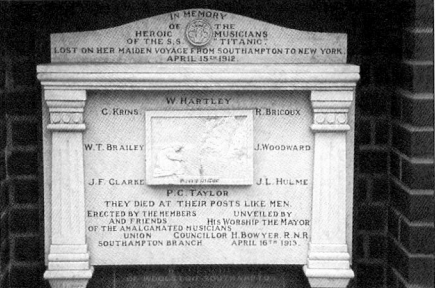

Peter Stone

**Titanic monuments, Southampton.
ABOVE: to the Engineer Officers.
BELOW: to the Musicians.**

who were lost to their families. Of the 1,500 people who were drowned, 549 were from Southampton. The memorials reflect their rank in life rather than their equality in death, each telling a version of the main event from the point of view of engineers, musicians, the crew on the lower deck and post office employees.

Mike Corbishley

Queen Victoria, Dovercourt, Essex.

Queen Victoria

There are almost certainly more memorials to Queen Victoria in the world than of any other person,

Mike Corbishley

Queen Victoria plaque on Coronation Villas, Tadcaster, North Yorkshire.

the majority commemorating her Diamond or Golden Jubilee rather than her death. The statues are all interesting studies in interpretation. Ask your pupils to look at

■ how the Queen is presented

■ the clothes she wears

■ any symbols of her office

■ the sentiments expressed in the inscriptions.

Look too for any references to the British Empire over which she reigned. Some communities celebrated the jubilees by erecting buildings which were public amenities such as bandstands, assembly rooms, art galleries, public parks and even clocks.

Fire of London by Sir Christopher Wren included a statue of Charles II on the top.

Statues erected to anti-slavery campaigners, to industrialists, inventors and explorers survive in large cities. Many public statues commemorate unexpected and disastrous events. In Southampton and the surrounding area there are eight memorials to the Titanic, which went down in 1912, and another in Liverpool. Stories of the Titanic tend to focus on the fate of the passengers, but in these maritime cities it is the crew members

Inscriptions

Inscriptions on all public statues and the style of lettering should be meticulously recorded. Back at school you can use the record to do follow-up or extension work. Inscriptions often provide information not just about the person in the statue and their achievements but on how the money for the erection of the statue was raised. Some of the details can be researched in reference books or in the local paper to fill out the story behind the statue. Lettering styles can become a topic in its own right, particularly for students of art and design as can a study of the symbols that appear on both large and small memorials.

Ken Glen

Memorial at Stokesay Church, Shropshire.

English Heritage

Street name, Leicester.

PLACE, STREET AND BUILDING NAMES

A lot of thought and discussion usually precedes the naming of streets and schools. A check on early Ordnance Survey maps and in directories (see page 29) may confirm the view that many of the streets, squares and buildings were named after Victoria, Albert

Mike Corbishley

House at Brantham, Suffolk recording the coronation of Edward VIII.

and their family and were chosen after Albert's death in 1861 or the Queen's Golden and Diamond Jubilees in 1887 and 1897. Not all local dignitaries are as nationally famous as Joseph Chamberlain, whose name was used for streets and squares in central Birmingham but you may uncover names of streets and buildings in your own locality selected as a sign of respect to a local alderman, mayor or

BELOW: A terrace of houses at Tadcaster, North Yorkshire.

Mike Corbishley

councillor after their death.

In some cases their achievements may now be forgotten so it would be a relevant study for a class to select their local dignitary as the subject for a local history investigation, particularly if their name is also the name of a local school. Newspaper reports and obituaries would be a main source of information (see page 29).

MEMORIAL BUILDINGS

Philanthropy was greatly admired in Victorian society and there are many examples of buildings erected from legacies left by the industrialists who made their fortunes in the nineteenth century. Education was one cause with which benefactors wished to be associated, and the new civic universities in particular, benefitted. Libraries, lecture theatres, halls of residence and other buildings were named after them. Two examples are the Wills Memorial Building at Bristol University named after the tobacco family and the Trent Building at Nottingham University, named after Jesse Boot, first Lord Trent, whose memorial bust stands outside the main gates of University Park.

BELOW: The Tate Public Library, Brixton, London in the 1890s.

London Borough of Lambeth Archives Department

Foundation stones
Look out for foundation stones or plaques on buildings, especially non-conformist chapels and public buildings.

Mike Corbishley

Mike Corbishley

A memorial to the Tolpuddle Martyrs.

Dreadnought Seaman's Hospital Greenwich, plaque in one of the wards.

Sir Bevil Grenville's Monument at Lansdown, Avon.

FOLLIES, CAIRNS AND MOUNTAIN MEMORIALS

In mountain or hill-walking areas you often come across memorials to former guides or ramblers such as that on Catbells in the Lake District, one of the first fells inexperienced walkers are encouraged to tackle.

Thomas Arthur Leonard, Founder of Co-operative and Communal Holidays and Father of the Open Air Movement of this country.
Born London March 12th 1864; Died Conway July 19th 1948. He believed that the best things that any mortal hath are those things which every mortal shares. He endeavoured to promote 'joy in widest commonality spread'.

Only a few schools will be prepared to climb a mountain to make a recording of a monument, but other memorials placed on significant vantage points, dominate the landscape for miles around. Some of these are no more than follies, buildings that, deceptively, look substantial from afar. The Ashton memorial (1906) in Lancaster was put up by Lord Ashton, in memory of his wife. It is an Italian baroque style temple.

PLAQUES ON BUILDINGS

Plaques are smaller and less imposing than many of the memorials already listed. Many record people who once lived in a particular house such as the well-known Blue Plaques. However, look out for those that provide details of events, as these can also be followed up in secondary sources. Exceptional tragic events within living memory that have been remembered on plaques include the disastrous fire at Hillsborough Football stadium in Sheffield and the terrorist bomb which killed two children in Warrington. Some plaques from the past have been removed from their original location and some have been destroyed in urban development schemes. The recording of memorials in vulnerable areas could be undertaken by any school or class as a project. Some developers are more sensitive than others. Sainsbury, for example, chose to place a plaque on their Guildford store recording the old inn that once stood on the site and the outside wall of their supermarket in Colchester records events from the town's history.

MEMORIALS OF BATTLES

Memorials were often put up to commemorate the site of a battle or a particular soldier. Sir Bevil Grenville's Monument at Lansdown in Avon records the heroism of a Royalist commander and his Cornish pikemen at the Battle of Lansdown.
(See Bibliography and Resources for further details on using the resource of battlefields).

BELOW: The Memorial Cross on the site of the Battle of Flodden Field, 1513, Northumberland.

ABOVE RIGHT: Blue plaque

RIGHT: Plaque on The Watch House, Hampstead.

English Heritage

Entrance to the Arboretum, Derby given to the town in 1840 by Joseph Strutt.

WAR MEMORIALS

Almost every town and village has a war memorial commemorating the dead of the two World Wars. They are dignified monuments erected by ordinary communities usually through public subscriptions, in response to the carnage of the First World War which affected almost every family in the land. The memorials were intended as a focus for the bereaved, most of whom would never travel to the real war graves and memorials in France and Belgium.

Many local newspapers of the time referred to them as peace memorials not war memorials, terms which can be discussed with pupils since they are an indication of public feelings of the time. It may also be necessary to distinguish the two wars with their dates, for younger pupils, particularly as in most cases new memorials were not put

Mike Corbishley

Funeral of the Unknown Warrior.

BELOW: The Cenotaph, Whitehall, London, taken in 1921.

PARKS AND GARDENS

The control and re-ordering of nature as parks or gardens was an eighteenth-century fashion with the wealthy land owning classes. Statues, mock temples and urns were installed in the landscape, although only rarely were they real memorials to real people. The exception is the Stowe Landscape Gardens in Buckinghamshire which is full of memorials to people and events. In the nineteenth century, the idea of a park as an amenity was extended to ordinary people, particularly in the towns and cities. Statues, fountains, bandstands, gates and park benches to commemorate real people and events became a feature, even in some cases while they were still alive.

Lister Park in Bradford is one such example. The donor, Samuel Lister, Lord Mayor and major woollen manufacturer, was present when his statue was unveiled in May 1875. It records in visual panels on the plinth the mechanisation of wool-combing, a patented invention which brought the town prosperity. In the park stands Cartwright Hall and Art Gallery, built in 1904 in the grounds of Lister's old home and named after Edmund Cartwright (1743-1823) a clergyman whom Lister admired since he invented a power loom at the height of the Industrial Revolution in 1784.

Royal Commission on Historical Monuments of England

ABOVE: Memorial to the members of staff of the Great Western Railway.
LEFT: Boer War Memorial, Shrewsbury, dedicated to the Militia and Volunteer Batallion of the King;'s Shropshire Light Infantry (Natal and Transvaal Wars 1899-1902)
RIGHT: First World War memorial in Abbey Park, Leicester by Lutyens.

ABOVE: Memorial dedicated to 'the Excellent Men and Women of Shropshire who fought in the wars of 1914-18 and 1939-45', Shrewsbury.
RIGHT: War memorial at Greengates, West Yorkshire.
BELOW: Model village for people disabled in the last war, Allenton near Derby. Plaque inset.

up after the Second World War, but names were added. In rare cases there may be residents still alive who can remember the memorial being unveiled. This may be an opportunity for pupils to carry out some oral history work.

Every community put great thought into the design of the memorial and local opinion was often divided on whether the memorial should be distinctively Christian, in the form of a cross, or secular with statues of soldiers in uniform. You may be able to catch some of the underlying debate about the form of the memorial in the local newspaper or any surviving programmes of commemoration that have survived in the local studies collections. War memorials still evoke feelings of anger at the waste of young peoples lives, particularly when it is evident from the inscriptions that several members of the same family were sacrificed.

One town which decided to commemorate the fallen on the streets where they actually lived was St Albans. Plaques, were erected on the walls of each street, providing evidence of the scale of the sacrifices made by families in one small area.

War memorials can be found in places other than the street. Schools, firms and railway companies often put up their own tribute and many of these are still to be added to the National Inventory of War Memorials being compiled at the Imperial War Museum (see page 36).

English Heritage

Mike Corbishley

Mike Corbishley

Mike Corbishley

TOP LEFT: City Centre Leeds.
TOP CENTRE: Memorial to a Victoria Cross holder, Walton-on-the-Naze, Essex.
TOP RIGHT: Air Force memorial Walton
LEFT: Kirby-le-Soken, Essex.
RIGHT: Navy memorial, Dovercourt, Essex.
BELOW LEFT: Midland Railway Memorial, Derby commemorating railway workers who lost their lives in the First World War.
BELOW CENTRE: The Carillon, Loughborough has 22 bells played on a keyboard.
BELOW RIGHT: The Soldier's memorial York.

ABOVE: Roose, Barrow-in-Furness, Cumbria.

Mike Corbishley

English Heritage

English Heritage

Mike Corbishley

MEMORIAL HALLS

Some communities decided not to erect monuments as a focus for their mourning in 1918 but to provide a more fitting memorial in the form of a building, such as a village hall, for those who had survived. Many were named the Memorial Hall and foundation stones or plaques record that the money was raised by public subscription. One particularly fine example of a memorial hall can be seen in the village of Balcombe in Sussex, where an artist was commissioned to paint a series of murals on the themes of war, peace and reconciliation.

ABOVE: War memorial, Colchester, Essex, unveiled in Empire Day 1923.
LEFT: Machine gunners memorial, Hyde Park Corner, London.

Extension work: War poetry

You may wish to extend work on war memorials by looking at other forms of evidence for war and people's attitudes to it. One of the most extraordinary aspects of the First World War in Britain was an upsurge in the writing of poetry.

It has been estimated that one and a half million war poems were written in August 1914 - that is 50,000 a day. Rupert Brooke evoked the spirit of the times with his famous poem *The Soldier*, written in 1914,

> If I should die, think only this of me:
>   That there's some corner of a foreign field
> That is for ever England. There shall be
>   In that rich earth a richer dust concealed;
> A dust whom England bore, shaped, made aware,
>   Gave, once, her flowers to love, her ways to roam,
> A body of England's, breathing English air,
>   Washed by the rivers, blest by suns of home.
>
> And think, this heart, all evil shed away,
>   A pulse in the eternal mind, no less
>   Gives somewhere back the thoughts by England
>   given;
>   Her sights and sounds; dreams happy as her day;
>   And laughter, learnt of friends; and gentleness,
>   In hearts at peace, under an English heaven.

Much of Wilfrid Owen's poetry concerns the appalling shared experiences of men formally cast as enemies. In *Strange Meeting*, partly quoted below, he imagines the experience of one soldier killed in war confronting another dead soldier from the same war. The poem finishes like this

> I am the enemy you killed, my friend.
> I knew you in this dark; for so you frowned
> Yesterday through me as you jabbed and killed.
> I parried; but my hands were loath and cold.
> Let us sleep now....

The memorial (below right) to Wilfrid Owen was commissioned from Paul de Monchaux in 1993 and stands in Shrewsbury where Owen lived from 1907. The sculpture expresses the significance of the poet as bridge builder and communicator and the stark shape reflects the structure of the trenches lined with duckboards. It also speaks of the Sambre Canal and the pontoon bridge which Owen's unit was struggling to construct when he was killed in November 1918.

You might also like to consider the work of poets of other countries as a contrast. One of the most interesting for pupils is the work of Guillaume Apollinaire, who died in November 1918 of influenza after he had been invalided out of the French army when a shell fragment pierced his right temple through his steel helmet. Below is a translation of *The Coffin and the Bed*.

```
            HERE
          IS THE C
          OFFIN IN
          WHICH H
          E REST
           ED RO
           TTING
           ANDP
           A L E


     LONG LIVE FRANCE!
     HE SLEEPS IN HIS LI
     TTLE SOLDIER'S BED
     MY   RESUSCITATED
     P                O
     E                T
```

English Heritage

British Museum

OBJECTS

Many objects commemorating events and people can be found in personal and museum collections. They are not all memorials to death. In 1588, Queen Elizabeth I ordered a gold medal to be struck to commemorate the victory over the Spanish Armada. Pottery, such as Delftware was used to commemorate the coronation of William and Mary, Staffordshire slipware by Thomas Toft and porcelain from Lowestoft records marriages and births.

Gold lockets with the hair of children and young women were popular in Victorian and Edwardian times and are a reminder of the frequency of death in the family and that many people died as children or young adults.

Needlework

Rarer, because they were domestic objects, are memorials to people and events in needlework. One in the collection of the Royal School of Needlework has the following inscription

There was an earthquake on the 8 September 1692 in the city of London but no hurt tho it caused most part of England to tremble.

In the eighteenth and early nineteenth century young girls designed their own samplers and one fashion was to make a record of the family history including the deaths of siblings and, in extreme cases their mothers. There is at least one needlework memorial to the sinking of the Titanic in the Maritime Museum in Southampton.

British Museum

First World War Medals

Commemorative medals were used by all parties in the great conflict as propaganda. Many, like this one (above), portrayed death in its stark reality. This German medal, designed by W Eberbach, shows a colossal skeleton in a devastated landscape. The activity is explained by the legend, 'Verdun, the world blood pump 1916'

The war at sea was also a favourite subject for medals during the First World War. The sinking of the Cunard liner, the Lusitania, by a German submarine in May 1915 saw a flurry of propaganda. Karl Goetz produced a medal which showed people queuing at a Cunard office, served by a skeleton, with the sign above 'Business above all'. The other side of the medal is headed 'No contraband' with the Lusitania overflowing with weapons and aircraft.

The English reaction to this was to put their own point of view by producing copies of the medal in a box (above).

TREES

Concern for the environment as well as a desire to commemorate a life or an event by a living memorial has resulted in the planting of individual trees or even whole avenues. Look out for any indications in names such as Jubilee Oak, which might have been planted for one of Victoria's jubilees or for the Silver Jubilee of Queen Elizabeth II.

Making memorials

Once your class has investigated actual memorials, you might like to encourage them to design and make their own, for example

■ read about a famous person from the past and design a suitable memorial, deciding where it might best be built

■ design a memorial for a real (or imaginary) ex-pupil

■ or you could use the shapes and forms of memorials to design and make an unusual chess set.

CEMETERIES AND MEMORIALS

His talents and industry, guided by integrity and honour, raised him to high distinction as a merchant. He was the first Mayor of Bradford in 1847. He represented the town in two successive Parliaments with fidelity and diligence. He was generous and warm hearted in his hospitalities, liberal in his support of religious and benevolent institutions. He departed this life in the faith and hope of the Gospel, 1st July 1862, aged 75.

Inscription on the tomb of Robert Milligan (1787-1862), Undercliffe Cemetery, Bradford.

RIGHT: The Robert Milligan monument.

Until the beginning of the nineteenth century everyone had the common law right to be buried in the churchyard of the parish where they died. The priest had an obligation to perform a burial service for anyone who had been baptised (which was most people) and to charge a burial fee. The exception was for suicides.

A number of factors led to the establishment of graveyards and cemeteries which gradually replaced the village churchyard as the customary place of burial.

DISSENTERS' BURIAL GROUNDS

Nonconformist ministers were not allowed to conduct services in an Anglican churchyard, and so many groups of dissenters bought land and opened burial grounds of their own. The Quakers were the first groups to do this and some fine examples of early eighteenth-century burial grounds, with chapels, can be found.

PRESSURES FOR NEW BURIAL GROUNDS

The industrial revolution brought a number of different problems. First there was a massive movement of population from the country into the expanding cities. Population in

RIGHT: Quaker Meeting House and burial ground, Bury St. Edmunds, Suffolk.

English Heritage

general also grew, so that even where churchyards existed in city centres, they became seriously overcrowded. Burial was the only legal way of disposing of dead bodies until the first modern cremation in 1901. Overcrowding presented a

health hazard, which became a cause for concern of the Chadwick Commissions set up to look into sanitary conditions in the 1840s. As a result, burial became regulated by a series of Burial Acts.

The solution was to establish the Victorian cemetery, which became a familiar landscape feature on the outskirts of most towns. Their design, buildings and memorials are a record of the wealth, values, taste and achievements of middle-class Victorian society.

VICTORIAN CEMETERY DESIGN

The first large cemeteries were built, not by local authorities, but by joint stock companies, as an investment. Shrewd entrepreneurs realised that the nouveaux-riches who had benefited financially from industrialisation would be happy to pay large sums to have their wealth and position in society displayed after death, just as the aristocracy had done inside churches in the preceding centuries. Respectability was granted to the Cemetery Movement, as it became known, when Augustus Frederick, sixth son of George III and his sister Princess Sophia took plots on the

Mike Corbishley

main avenue of Kensal Green Cemetery in London. Unlike churchyards, cemeteries were deliberately designed with the funeral ceremony in mind. They were walled and owe something to the landscaped parks favoured by the gentry in the eighteenth century. Fashionable and successful architects were employed to design elaborate gatehouses at the entrance to the cemetery, chapels (for different denominations), avenues of differing proportions, landscaped areas, tree plantations and even some of the monuments themselves. Catacombs, where coffins were placed but not interred, were a design feature in several places.

All Victorian cemeteries were designed with a grand central avenue, generally leading from the gatehouse to the chapel. The largest memorials, housing the wealthiest citizens, are likely to be along this central avenue, simply because families were invited to buy plots, from a prepared plan, just as on newly-built housing estates today.

In some cemeteries, areas were reserved for particular social groups, so that in Cambridge, for example, there is a designated 'University' space. In others, style of tomb or mausoleum dictated where people were buried, the most famous being the Egyptian Avenue

Gravestone in Histon cemetery, Cambridge.

in Highgate cemetery. People without money to buy a plot were buried on the perimeters of the cemetery and the very poor in mass, unmarked graves.

INTERPRETING MEMORIALS

Many of these are examples of ostentation and display as well as reflections of sentiment and loss. Once a family bought a plot, their decendants continued to be buried there for the next hundred years or more. In some cases the family

BELOW:Funerary urn at Ramsey, Essex.

BELOW RIGHT: Guardian angel at Dovercourt, Essex.

Urn and broken weeping willow tree.

bought a mausoleum, rather than a plot. These are like small chapels. Coffins covered in lead, were placed on shelves in the mausoleum, not interred.

You are more likely to find the addresses of wealthy Victorians on memorials in cemeteries, than on headstones in graveyards. This will enable you to follow up an investigation in street directories and census returns. Funerary sculpture followed fashion just like the building of houses, schools and churches in Victorian times. In rough chronological order these were

■ Neo-Classical or Georgian (columns, urns, domes)

■ Egyptian, inspired by knowledge of the Egyptian way of death gained during the Napoleonic wars,(obelisks, sun images, papyrus and sphinxes)

■ Victorian Gothic (Eleanor crosses, pinnacles)

■ Many guardian angels will be found on Victorian memorials. These do not fit into any of the

London Cemeteries
In the early part of the nineteenth century there were 52,000 funerals in London each year. A bill was passed in 1832 in Parliament for 'Establishing a General cemetery for the Interment of the Dead in the Neighbourhood of the Metropolis'. This cemetery was Kensal Green Cemetery. Other large cemeteries were soon opened, for example,

■ Norwood 1838

■ Highgate 1839

■ Abney Park 1840

■ Brompton 1840

■ Tower Hamlets 1841

stylistic categories above, but were influenced by images in Italian paintings of the Renaissance.

FAMOUS PEOPLE

Even famous people in the Victorian and Edwardian periods were buried in the local cemetery. Industrialists, engineers,inventors, Members of Parliament, entertainers, philanthropists and reformers whom pupils read about in school text books are all buried somewhere. Their memorials often provide a sentence or two about the reasons for their fame.

STONE MASONS

Only the very rich could afford to commission sculpture from an artist. Some excellent individual pieces were the work of local stone masons. Many wisely set up their yards and showrooms near the cemetery gate and remain in business today, despite the move from interment to cremation. Look, as you enter the cemetery, for any information on the stonemasons shop front about the date of origin. In the past, as today, most relatives chose their gravestones and decorative features off the peg from samples in the yard or, in exceptional cases, from a catalogue.

Highgate Cemetery

The London Cemetery Company bought land at Highgate for £3,500. A Parliamentary Act of 1836 gave the company permission to build three cemeteries (in Surrey, Kent and Middlesex). The sloping meadows which the company had bought at Highgate, were changed into a landscaped park by the founder of the company Stephen Geary, who was himself an architect. He was assisted by David Ramsey, a landscape gardener and J B Bunning, an architect.

The whole area was accessible by winding paths but the most extraordinary feature was the Egyptian Avenue, the reserve of the wealthiest citizens - a vault here cost 130 guineas in 1878. This area was created by cutting out the steepest part of the hillside. The entrance to this exclusive part of the cemetery was

TOP LEFT: The Circle of Lebanon.
TOP CENTRE: Memorials with draped urns.
ABOVE LEFT: Entrance to the Egyptian Avenue.
ABOVE CENTRE: Memorial to George Wombwell.

ABOVE: Pyramid memorial; Broken column; The empty chair.
(Photos: English Heritage)

through an iron gateway under an enormous Pharaonic arch with obelisks on each side.

Another unusual feature at Highgate is the Circle of Lebanon. There were twenty vaults here facing a circular island of earth on which grows a large cedar tree. This was such a favourite place for burial that another forty vaults were constructed in an outer circle.

The third of Highgate's special features was the Terrace Catacombs. An underground gallery held 840 separate recesses - each for a single coffin. Many people chose to keep their

deceased in the Catacombs only for as long as it took to design and build a tomb or mausoleum.

Highgate Cemetery began to fall into disrepair during the Second World War. In 1975 United Cemeteries Ltd, which had bought out the original company, paid off most of its employees. The Friends of Highgate Cemetery was formed and set up a Trust to buy and maintain the cemetery. In 1981 a company formed by two Friends of Highgate Cemetery bought the cemetery for £50.

TOP LEFT: Memorials with wheelcrosses and urns.
CENTRE LEFT: The Quaker Burial Ground.
BOTTOM LEFT: The Illingworth Mausoleum.
ABOVE CENTRE: The Holden family tomb.
ABOVE RIGHT: The historic core of the Undercliffe Cemetery with the Swithen Anderton monument to the left, a scaled down version of the Scott memorial in Edinburgh.
BELOW: The Promenade with views over Bradford.
(Photos: English Heritage)

Undercliffe Cemetery, Bradford

In 1852 the Bradford Cemetery Company was registered, having bought a large plot of land in Undercliffe. The cemetery was designed by William Gay, who had previously been the registrar of the Leicester Cemetery. The first burials took place in 1854. The cemetery is terraced and it was along the terrace walk that Bradford's most important citizens wanted to build their mausolea.

The cemetery is divided, east-west, into two areas, each with its own mortuary chapel. One area was for the non-conformists - Quakers, Methodists and Baptists. The other area was consecrated for Church of England burials. There are over 23,000 graves in Undercliffe, probably representing 123,000 interments.

By 1977 burials at Undercliffe had declined and the Bradford Cemetery Company was liquidated. The site became neglected and vandalised. When a property developer bought the cemetery (for £5!), local people became concerned about the removal of buildings, walls, trees and gravestones. They formed The Friends of Undercliffe Cemetery and campaigned for its rescue. Bradford Metropolitan Council compulsorily purchased the cemetery and sponsored a three-year restoration programme. In 1986 a new Bradford Undercliffe Cemetery Company was formed which promotes the site as 'a place of special interest and to guarantee its continuance as a place of burial.'

RECORDING CHURCH AND CATHEDRAL MEMORIALS

In youth she was most lovely,
In womanhood most dignified,
In old age most venerable.
It was truly said of her in her prime
That it was difficult which to admire most
The beauty of her virtue or the virtue
of her beauty.
In her breast were united the tenderness of
an Englishwoman And the spirit of a
Roman matron.
The faculties and endowments of her mind
were of the highest order
Her opinions, her principles, all the senti-
ments of her heart Were sincere, upright
and noble. Her whole life was that of a
real Christian Pious without austerity and
charitable without ostentation
May I die the death of the righteous
And may my latter end be like hers.

To Agnetta Yorke, who died December 1820
aged 81. St Andrew's Church,
Wimpole, Cambridgeshire.

Churches and churchyards provide opportunities for pupils to study memorials at first hand, to record what they see and to collect data that can later be analysed in school.

WHAT TO LOOK FOR

Burials or memorials inside a church or cathedral were for the rich and privileged, such as the clergy, the local gentry, church benefactors or public servants. You may find examples on the walls and floor of a church, inside chapels, as stained glass windows or as objects.

Brasses

Examples of memorial brasses can be found in churches in most counties. They date from between the thirteenth and the fifteenth century and commemorate local knights, landholders or church benefactors. By the late fourteenth and early fifteenth centuries many of these were merchants who had profited from the trade in wool. Brasses originated in northern France and Flanders.

The alloy of brass used for the sheets was a different composition

IMPORTANT

Before embarking on any recording work, check out the regulations. Sometimes flash photography is not allowed inside a church or cathedral and brasses should never be rubbed without written permission. Gravestones and monuments outside often have lichen growing on them. Unfortunately this gravestone at Newton Kyme, North Yorkshire has had the lichen rubbed off to read a name. See Churchyard ecology page 26 for details on carrying out a school project.

Brasses in the church at Orford, Suffolk.

from modern brass and made from 75% copper, 19% zinc, 2% of tin and 4% of lead. Before engraving the design was drawn out and copied on to the sheet of metal in paint or with a pointed tool. The lines were then engraved. A recess of the exact size was made in the floor of the church. Today many brasses have been removed to the wall for preservation. Brasses are a good source for projects on

■ clothes and fashion

■ armour and weapons

■ heraldry.

You can also research the history of the person seen in effigy and their place in the neighbourhood. Taking an imprint of the effigy as a brass rubbing was very popular, until their fragility was recognised. Permission must be obtained in writing nowadays before any rubbing is done. For this reason, excellent reproductions of many brasses have now been made in fibre glass and many towns and cities have a brass rubbing centre where all equipment is provided and school parties may rub facsimile brasses from all over the country.

Tombs

Normally, the oldest tombs inside a church or cathedral belong to clergy or to royalty as they were the only people who had a right to be buried there. Demand for this privilege from influential landowners and wealthy citizens increased, particularly just before and during the Reformation. Many were prepared to give generously to the church when alive for a space inside once they died. The monument in death became a substitute for display in life and, in churches and cathedrals with a lot of tombs, a chronological survey of taste and fashion can be made. Table tombs are the largest, many with portrait effigies of the people buried beneath. Look for symbols of office and social position, such as a crozier or a coat of arms. Post-Reformation priests and wealthy merchants from the Tudor period showed off their large families at a period in history when marriage of the clergy was first sanctioned and became respectable.

The eighteenth century is probably the greatest period for exuberance and extravagance in tomb design. Some of the greatest sculptors of the age, such as Rysbrack, Flaxman and Banks, were commis-

Memorial in St Mary's Church, Berry Pomeroy, Someset.

sioned by families whose wealth had increased through colonial expansion and trade. The influence of classical architecture that can be seen in all large country houses of the period was extended into the memorials for the dead. Look out for

■ lengthy eulogies, often in Latin

■ drapery

■ columns

■ symbols of death and mourning like skulls and spent hour glasses.

In village churches near a great house, a series of tombs can often be used to construct family trees and family histories, since many record the names of the surviving members of the family who erected the tomb. There are fewer tombs from Victorian times partly because of the lack of space and partly because it was more fashionable to show off in death with a large tomb in a public cemetery or in a prominent position in a churchyard.

Stained glass

The use of stained glass windows as memorials is a comparatively recent idea, but many examples can be found in urban and rural churches as well as in large cathedrals. Stained glass was used in the general building trade in Victorian and Edwardian times in houses, town halls, office buildings, schools and colleges and railway stations. Many of the memorial windows in churches were made by local craftworkers whose skills survived through the 1920s and 1930s when stained glass remained a feature of many suburban houses. The church guide will reveal if you are lucky enough to have windows designed by a famous artist or designer, whose artistic output can become the subject of an investigation as well as the people commemorated in the window. William Morris and Company were commissioned to make a number of memorial windows from the 1880s and in the twentieth century artists such as John Piper.

Most memorial windows were donated by families but some commemorate groups of local people, including those lost in war.

One of the most recent memorial windows to be commissioned and set up was one to Oscar Wilde in Poet's Corner, Westminster Abbey. (see opposite page) The Dean of Westminster, Reverend Michael Mayne, dedicated the window on 15 February 1995 and Sir John Gielgud delivered an extract from the artist's end-of-life meditation, *De Profundis*,

'I have altered the minds of men and the colours of things.
There was nothing I said or did that

LEFT: Tomb of Ralph Nevill, Earl of Westmorland, and his two wives. St Mary's Church, Staindrop, Durham.

Memorial pulpit in Tadcaster, North Yorkshire.

did not make people wonder. I showed that the false and the true are merely forms of intellectual existence.'

You might get your class to consider

■ what sort of subject might be suitable as an illustration for a stained glass window and compare it to, say a carved memorial

■ whether the form of a memorial window is more suitable in a public or private building.

Imitation stained glass windows can easily be made from coloured paper and attached to the inside of a classroom window.

Objects

Churches also contain objects donated by individual families or parishioners as memorials. One of the most popular gifts is a lectern or pulpit and, like the stained glass windows, some were commissioned from famous artists and designers. There may be an inscription on the lectern or further information in the church guide. Look also for embroidered hassocks. Occasions such as the Queen's Silver Jubilee are often marked by a collective community effort to provide something useful for the church.

Basic Latin

Although Latin ceased to be the language used in Church of England services and in the Bible at the time of the Reformation in the sixteenth century, it continued to be used on many tombs in churches. In the eighteenth century neo-classicism was the fashionable design style adopted by the gentry and nobility, particularly on their tombs. Point out to pupils that sometimes even the Latin words were abbreviated.

Latin	English
Hic jacet	Here lies
Obit Ob.	Died
Aetis sua aet.	At the age of
Requiescat in pace	RIP Rest in peace

Roman numerals
....were often used on memorials and gravestones:

I	1
II	2
III	3
IV	4
V	5
VI	6
VII	7
VIII	8
VIIII or IX	9
X	10
XI	11
XV	15
XX	20
XXX	30
XL	40
L	50
LX	60
LXX	70
XC	90
C	100
CC	200
CCC	300
CD	400
D	500
DC	600
DCC	700
CM	900
M	1000

RECORDING IN THE CHURCHYARD

We late-lamented, resting here,
Are mixed to human jam,
And each to each exclaims in fear,
'I know not which I am.'

Thomas Hardy, The Levelled Churchyard, 1882.

Churchyard in Manningtree, Essex with damaged tombs.

While no two churchyards are alike and each will have developed differently, there are similarities. The most striking will be the number of memorials inside a relatively small space - perhaps as many as 20 million surviving in this country today. The space in churchyards was limited. Burials had to be made in the same ground over and over again. Most medieval memorials have been lost and gravemarkers made of material such as wood have mostly been allowed to decay. Wood was used for simple markers but also for grave-rails and more elaborate structures often called bed-heads.

IMPORTANT

Always get permission to take your class, however small, to visit and to record the gravestones in a churchyard. You will need to be especially careful about going into areas

■ where burials still take place

■ graves which have regular visitors

■ areas set aside for wild plants.

Although there were greater numbers of gravestones made from the later sixteenth century, many graveyards contain few examples dated before about 1800.

It is important to make a permanent record of whole graveyards because many are under some sort of threat from

■ vandalism or neglect

■ either wholesale clearance

■ or partial clearance due to the parish authorities wishing to 'tidy-up' to allow easier grass-cutting.

However more communities are beginning to value their graveyards as a centre for the survival of plants, wildlife and habitats (see Bibliography and Resources). Some parishes have returned to the medieval practice of using animals - sheep, goats or geese - to keep the grass down. These issues can give rise to discussion about

■ the purpose of having marked graves at all

■ the cost of churchyard upkeep

■ environmental issues about the flora and fauna in churchyards.

BEFORE THE VISIT

It is a good idea to talk to your pupils, or allow them to discover for themselves the orientation of graveyards. You will want to discuss

■ what the main constituent parts of the church are (nave, chancel) as well as other features (such as a tower, porch, vestry and side chapels)

■ why the church has an east window behind the altar

You will also want to explain that the Christian burial involves orientation east-west. The corpse should

be buried to allow it to rise on the Day of Judgement facing to the east. This gives the opportunity to discuss the practice of other religions, both today and in the past.

It is also good idea to practise with any equipment you are going to use in the survey, such as tape measures and compasses.

Preparing an outline plan

Explain that recording a complete graveyard is important because the gravestones themselves, and especially their inscriptions, provide us with a wealth of historical evidence about the people who once lived there.

You should prepare an outline plan of the graveyard in advance of the visit to hand out to groups of pupils and to mark the position of each gravestone. The easiest way is to photocopy part of a map, increasing its size on a photocopier.

AT THE CHURCHYARD

After a general look round the churchyard, pupils may like to give their first impressions of the size of the graves, particularly those nearest to the church and give a

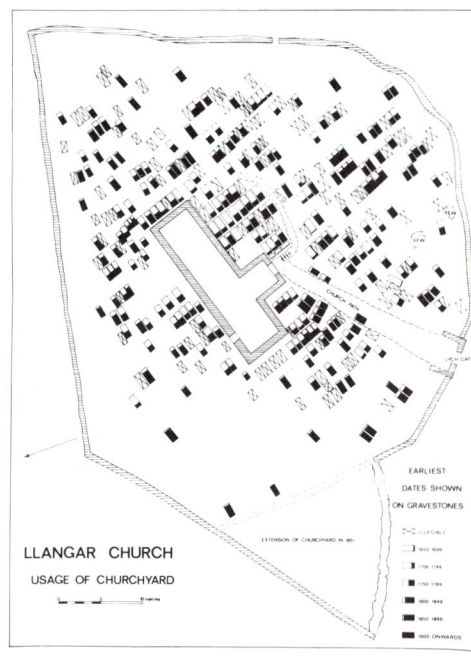

LLANGAR CHURCH
USAGE OF CHURCHYARD

EARLIEST DATES SHOWN ON GRAVESTONES

quick assessment of the age of most of them.

Recording the information on gravestones is important conservation work, particularly valuable for genealogy. Pupils can then be sent in pairs to collect data from individual gravestones using a gravestone recording sheet. A plan of the graveyard can be distributed for each pair to record where 'their' grave is located. An alternative activity is for one group to make a plan of the graveyard using measuring equipment as a preliminary to studying individual graves.

Making the plan

Take a fixed point to begin constructing your plan. The wall of the church, a path or boundary wall will be easy to work to. A base line should be set out 90° to it. Squares can then be set out with rods at 10m intervals. Gravestones can then be accurately measured in to each square.

Recording each memorial

Each memorial, whether a tomb or a gravestone, should be given an individual record number. You should record the following information

■ inscription

■ any decoration

■ shape of memorial

■ condition of memorial

and, if possible

■ type(s) of material used to make the memorial.

You can use a variety of recording methods such as

■ written record

■ taped record

■ drawn record

■ photographic record.

■ recording details on a small cassette recorder - especially useful for pupils with special educational needs.

You might want to discuss with your pupils which methods are the most appropriate for the study of memorials in the future.

Grave Memorial Recording Form

Your pupils could invent their own recording form or you could use the standard form developed by the Council for British Archaeology and RESCUE. An example of the form is reproduced and further details about the form and the accompanying book may be found on page 36.

Looking at the details

Inscriptions on gravestones are not always easy to read. Pupils may find the language difficult or the stone may be eroded or covered with lichen. Do not rub the gravestone or try to scratch where the letters may be - there are more effective ways. You could try

■ casting a shadow across the inscription using a coat (or take some black paper with you)

■ throwing strong light at an angle (using a torch or a mirror to reflect sunlight).

ANALYSING THE DATA

The data collected can be used back at school to build up a picture of families and communities.

Sequencing

All the graves in the churchyard can be collated into chronological order. The death of the first person named is likely to be the best indication of the date of the grave.

Location

Were there parts of the churchyard developed at particular decades in the past? Where were the largest graves located? Whose were they?

Family Trees

Do the gravestones provide data to draw some family trees ?

Mortality statistics

Select a fifty year period and make some graphs to show

■ age of death of males buried in the churchyard

■ age of death of females buried in the churchyard

■ deaths of infants and children.

Family size

Can any conclusions be drawn from the data about family size in the past?

First names

Make a graph to show the most popular first names of people who died during a specified period.

Occupations

Are any occupations given?

FROM TOP: Measuring triangulation using tape measures.
Casting angled light with bacofoil reflector.
Casting angled shadow to see lettering.
Recording by photography.

Epitaphs

Make a record of all the epitaphs or texts used on the gravestones and where they came from. You might want to discuss whether the evidence given on gravestones is sufficient to build up a picture of a person, a family or a community in the past. You could choose a gravestone known to your pupils to carry out this exercise. Your pupils could also design their own memorials. They could

■ choose a particular period to base it on

■ write a suitable epitaph

■ design a form of decoration which they think is most fitting

■ make up a catalogue for a gravestone manufacturer and design a suitable advertisement to go into the local newspaper.

Patches of lichen growing on a gravestone.

Symbols

Symbols in carving or statuary are often used on memorials to convey a message about attitudes to death or a reflection of religious beliefs. Many are very ancient in origin and can be found in portraits and in literature as well as on tombs and graves. Some are Christian, some secular and some classical in origin. Some of the most common symbols used on memorials and their meanings are

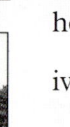

Symbol	Meaning
cross	believer in Christianity
angel	guardian - often points towards heaven
open book	faith
dove	The Holy Ghost or at peace
hands, clasped	farewell
heart	love and devotion
ivy	immortality, friendship
anchor	hope, rest - an early Christian symbol
obelisk	eternal life - from Egyptian worship of the sun
rocks	Christian, reliable and steadfast
hour glass/scythe	time/life has passed
laurel	fame
skull & crossed bones	mortality
broken column	the removal of support - often used for death of head of family
torch	immortality
torch upturned	life extinguished
willow	grief, mourning

A graveyard ecology survey

Divide the site so that the whole picture can be acquired at the end of the study, using a pre-prepared plan overlaid with a labelled grid.

Issue each pair of pupils with a standard school hoop, a clipboard and some plain paper on which a circle has already been drawn and given the graveyard grid reference. They will also need access to reference books on site.

Having identified their working area, ask your pupils to place their hoop on the ground in either full sun, partial sun or shade - noting which it is.

Ask them to map plants, using a key, on their circle and list any insects or other mini-beasts they find within their hoop and note any birds or mammals within their grid square.

Back at the classroom full-size circles can be cut out of white paper, the plant life mapped, with a key, and animal life listed. These could then form a display.

This activity could be developed into graph work - plotting the evidence for the most common plant, insect, bird or animal.

MEMORIALS IN THE LOCAL ENVIRONMENT

A study of memorials need not concentrate on the most famous, or the grandest, or those which involve travel for a school class. All the memorials listed below are within walking distance of one primary school in Cambridge.

Pub sign

This modern pub was named after the first overland crossing of Antarctica by Sir Vivian Fuchs' expedition on snow tractors. Ideas for follow-up might be to

■ describe the vehicle on the pub sign and its location

■ find out reason for name of pub by questions to publican and local people

■ look at old photographs on display inside pub

■ use reference books to find out more snow tractors and Vivian Fuchs' expedition in 1956

■ visit the local museum where a snow tractor is displayed.

Building foundation stone

This foundation stone of a modern church was laid by Princess Margaret. Pupils might

■ record information on stone by rubbing or drawing

■ make notes of architectural details and style of the church

■ note similarities and differences with an older church in the locality

■ find newspaper account and photograph of event at Local Studies library

■ ask local people for reminiscences about the occasion

■ use notes, drawings and other evidence to produce an information sheet for visitors to the church.

Street names

Several of the streets on a post-war housing estate near the school were named after generals of the Second World War. It might be interesting to

■ use the catalogue at the Local Studies Library or local knowledge about reasons for street names

■ use reference books to find out more about Second World War leaders commemorated in street names.

At the parish church

The churchyard at the parish church has examples of gravestones from the eighteenth century onwards but on an outside wall is an unusual dedica-

tion. Extension work on slavery could be carried out by

■ using a copy of the full inscription to write an account of the life of Anna Maria and her parents

■ investigating what happened to Africans who became slaves in the eighteenth century

■ finding out about the people who worked to make slavery illegal

■ finding out about Anna Maria's father, who wrote his own life story, using both his African name Olaudah Equiano and his European name Gustavus Vassa.

War Memorial

This war memorial is in the churchyard near the entrance to the church. Several questions could be posed to pupils

■ when was it erected?

■ when were new names added?

■ how many local people died in the First World War?

■ how many died in the Second World War?

■ can they recognise any local names?

■ are there any families who lost people in both wars?

■ how does the memorial make them feel?

Dog trough

The full inscription of this dog trough is

1934 In memory of Tony, a dog who gave him friendship and happiness during his Cambridge years. This trough is erected by His Royal Highness Prince Chula of Siam.

This unusual memorial might prompt several pieces of work such as

■ where was Siam?

■ what is it called today?

■ do a local survey to find out how many dogs use the trough today?

Alexandra Gardens

Activities might include

■ finding Queen Alexandra, who died in November 1925, on a family tree of the Royal family

■ writing to the City Council pointing out there is no information about her in the Gardens, and offer to design a suitable notice

■ searching in old newspapers for any report of the opening of the Gardens, after the Queen's death

■ asking anyone, born before 1925, what they remember about Queen Alexandra and the charity Alexandra Rose Day

■ incorporating all their information on the notice to go in the Gardens or in a leaflet.

Date plaques on houses

There are several names and dates on houses in the locality.
Pupils could

■ use the dates on the houses to draw a diagram or map to show the chronology of buildings in a chosen area

■ check out the streets and terraces on an Ordnance Survey map drawn about same time

■ use the street directories or census returns to find out who lived in the houses when they were first built.

Industrial Cottage, 1887

■ look in the census returns for 1881 and 1891 to find out who lived and worked here

■ find out what industry was carried on there by further research in the Local Studies Library.

Cemetery

There is a small Victorian cemetery laid out on Histon Road, similar in layout to the much grander ones in London or Bradford. Pupils could

■ record in drawing or photography symbols about life and death from the graves

■ construct some family trees from information on family plots

■ list the most popular first names of people who died before 1990, between 1900 and 1930 and between 1930 and 1960.

French's Road

This road contains a number of different types of memorials from the street name to inscriptions in a now re-used industrial complex. Pupils could be asked to

■ use buildings, date inscriptions and names along French's Road and on the old mill site work out what has changed over the last 100 years

■ talk to people living in French's Road about changes they remember

Borough Council Housing

THE 2000th HOUSE
BUILT BY THE BOROUGH OF CAMBRIDGE
1919-1934

Cambridge Borough Council were proud of their record of public housing to put up a memorial plaque. Pupils might

■ make a transcript of the plaque

■ use a street directory from 1934 to find out who lived in the house

■ put out an appeal for anyone who lived in the street at that time, asking them what the houses were like inside

■ discuss why it is important for councils to build houses to rent

■ find out who is on the Housing Committee today, asking them about commemorative plaques being put up today.

DOCUMENTS

*In memory of 67 individuals of various
ages and either sex who
in the short period from June 21st to
August 13th AD 1832 died
in this Rectory of ASIATIC CHOLERA, a
frightful and previously
unknown disease in this county. Reader!
Why hast thou been spared?
To what purpose has thou been left until
now?*

St Peter's Church, Upwell.

Stories behind memorials can be easily researched through some of the most accessible documents housed in the Local Studies Library or County Record Office.

NEWSPAPERS

Local newspapers are the first source of supporting information about events, individuals or families recorded on memorials. The date on the inscription is the starting point. There may be an account of a public unveiling ceremony which reveals who was present at the ceremony and how the money for the memorial was raised.

Extraordinary events in the history of the neighbourhood, such as the cholera epidemic mentioned above, mining disasters and other accidents will have been reported in the newspaper. Large monuments, such as those found in the main avenue of a Victorian cemetery fre-

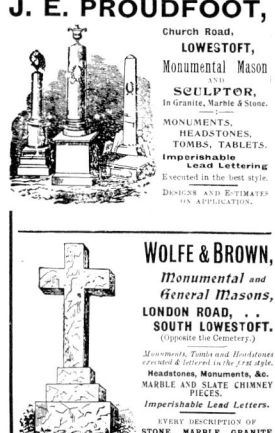

J. E. PROUDFOOT,
Church Road,
LOWESTOFT,
Monumental Mason
AND
SCULPTOR,
In Granite, Marble & Stone.

MONUMENTS,
HEADSTONES,
TOMBS, TABLETS.
Imperishable
Lead Lettering
Executed in the best style.

DESIGNS and ESTIMATES
ON APPLICATION.

WOLFE & BROWN,
Monumental and
General Masons,
LONDON ROAD, ..
SOUTH LOWESTOFT.
(Opposite the Cemetery.)

Monuments, Tombs and Headstones
erected & lettered in the first style.
Headstones, Monuments, &c.
MARBLE AND SLATE CHIMNEY
PIECES.
Imperishable Lead Letters.
EVERY DESCRIPTION OF
STONE, MARBLE, GRANITE
and SLATE WORK.

**Local trade directories
are good sources for
monuments and
buildings as well as
monumental masons**

quently belong to families or individuals whose death and funeral was reported in the newspaper, which may also carry an obituary notice. These provide information about the occupation, residence and relatives of the deceased as well as details of their activities in the community.

It is fairly easy to work out family relationships from the inscriptions but these are confirmed when death announcements and funeral particulars are turned up in the newspaper (below). The funeral reports also reveal that the family

FUNERAL OF MR. THODAY.

The remains of the late Mr F. Thoday, of Camden House, Hills-road, were laid to rest in the Histon-road Cemetery this (Thursday) after-noon. The Rev J. Jull, of Eden Chapel, con-ducted the service.

The principal mourners were Mr F. Thoday, Mr ...... Mr Sidney

FUNERAL OF MR HERBERT THODAY, OF CAMBRIDGE, THIS AFTERNOON.

Mr Herbert S. Thoday, after a lingering illness, expired on April 23rd, and this (Wednesday) after-noon, the interment took place at the Histon-road Cemetery. The deceased gentleman, who was a partner in the well-known building firm of Thoday and Son, took a deep interest in all kinds of sport, but was principally known for his connection with the N.S.A., with which body he was actively associated until his recent illness, having been on the Emergency Committee

DEATH OF MR. FRANCIS THODAY.

We regret to announce the death of Mr Francis Thoday, of Camden House, Hills-road, which took place at his residence on Saturday. Mr Thoday was well known as a builder and contractor, which business he carried on in the town for over 50 years. Deceased took no part in politics, and but for having been one of the original directors of the Cambridge Tramways Co., had been unconnected with public life. He resigned this office over 10 years ago, and six years ago he retired from business. The last work he personally took in hand was the erection of the new part of the Guildhall. He was the owner of a considerable amount of property. He leaves a widow and two daughters. The funeral will take place on Thurs-day at Histon-road Cemetery.

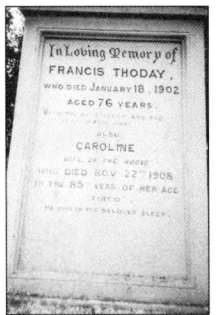

LEFT: Thoday family tomb.

In 1923 a memorial was erected to the men of Colchester who gave their lives in the Great War; 1914-18; it includes a pedestal of Portland stone surmounted by statues of Victory, St. George and of Peace: the site was provided by Viscount and Viscountess Cowdray, who gave £10,000 for the purchase of Colchester Castle, and a further £15,000 for the purchase of the Holly Trees mansion and adjoining property, so that the memorial might stand in the cleared space opposite All Saints' church with the castle in the background.

were local builders and connections made to a local street name, in an area developed around 1880. Further research, using an index in the library, finds deeds of houses built and subsequently sold by the two brothers.

CENSUS RETURNS

We have already shown that in some cases people have their addresses inscribed on their graves, particularly where such an address identifies social and economic status. In the case of the Thoday family, such details were found in the newspaper reports of the funeral. The address of the first deceased could be followed up in the census returns, since he died before 1891. Census returns remain confidential for 100 years, but where available contain details of all members of the household, including lodgers and servants.

STREET DIRECTORIES

Although not as detailed as census returns, street directories list householders and, sometimes, their occupations. This would enable us to put the Thodays into a social and occupational context. You will also find lists of monumental masons and, sometimes, their advertisements. Ordnance Survey maps of the area when they lived there would fill out the story of their domestic circumstances when alive.

Street directories may also list public memorials, such as war memorials.

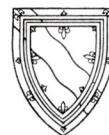

CAMBRIDGESHIRE WAR MEMORIAL

UNVEILING BY

H.R.H. THE DUKE OF YORK, K.G.

OF THE MONUMENT IN HILLS ROAD, CAMBRIDGE, ERECTED IN HONOUR OF THE MEN OF CAMBRIDGESHIRE, THE ISLE OF ELY, THE BOROUGH AND UNIVERSITY OF CAMBRIDGE, WHO SERVED IN THE WAR 1914–1919

PROGRAMMES

Programmes were often published for significant events such as the unveiling and dedication of a war memorial. These not only give some details of the people invited to be present, but of the architect and of the ceremony itself. In some cases there may also be a press photograph of the event, although this was not as easy as it is today, and certainly unlikely for anything unveiled before 1900.

ARCHITECTS' PLANS

Drawings and plans for large public memorials have probably survived in the Local Studies Library or the Record Office. These are doubly interesting if several designs were submitted, as often happened with a public commission like a war memorial, and only one chosen. Plans may also exist for cemeteries and chapels.

CEMETERY REGISTERS

Every burial had to be recorded by law in a register of the cemetery, with a note of the plot number. It was customary to deposit the register in the cemetery lodge and unfortunately many disappeared, but registers of death can be traced through the national archive at St Catherine's House. Books on family history provide details of how to make a search.

EARLY LITHOGRAPHS AND PHOTOGRAPHS

Visual material about memorials are not prolific, but since the cemetery was seen as an amenity and a place to take a walk dressed in 'Sunday' best in Victorian and Edwardian times, some early lithographs and photographs from the period survive.

A cheap and easy way of gathering visual evidence is from old postcards. Subjects like war memorials were popular in the past. You could ask your pupils to gather examples from family archives but you could also look in second-hand book shops, junk shops and antique shops. You may even find some foreign examples.

BELOW: The unveiling of a statue to King Edward VII at Tooting Broadway, London; 4 November 1911.

Case Study: A village war memorial

One school did a project based on their local war memorial.
They began by making a visit. On this visit they worked in groups and

■ recorded the inscription and all the names of the dead

■ took Polaroid photos

■ made drawings

■ recorded its general appearance and upkeep

■ marked the memorial's location on a map.

Back at school they began to work out why the village had placed the memorial where it was, asking questions such as

■ the most prominent position?

■ why not in the churchyard like some other villages in the neighbourhood?

■ the only position they could choose?

With the information about the war memorial recorded, the teacher followed up by asking the pupils to ask their relatives for

■ any information they had about the building of the memorial

■ any photographs of the memorial in the past

■ any photographs of people who were listed on the memorial.

The teacher also checked the entries in the street directory and asked the Clerk to the Parish Council for copies of the relevant entries for the memorial when it was discussed at Council meetings.
Then village residents were selected to be interviewed by pupils about the building of the memorial and their attitudes to it

now. Extension work was also carried out into the effect of world wars on a small village community, comparing the number of 'the fallen' with the population of the village in 1914 and 1939.
Linked to a graveyard survey they followed up by checking the names of the war dead with other family graves. They also found an official war gravestone.

TOP: Family portrait brought in by one of the pupils.

ABOVE: The memorial in 1946 at the time it was re-dedicated to the dead of the Second World War.

LEFT: The original dedication ceremony in 1920.

ISSUES ABOUT MEMORIALS

'One gets the feeling that some of these people would rather do away with memorials altogether; after all they get in the way of the mower.'

Letter to the editor, The Independent, 8 November 1993.

Issues about the preservation of memorials, their cost and value appear frequently in the news.

CONSERVATION

The parish council is often the place where views are heard about tidying up churchyards or removing gravestones when it is believed no survivors of the deceased are still alive. There now exists a considerable body of support for the conservation of Victorian cemeteries from conservation society members and others. The publication of cemetery trails and open days show that there is now a considerable interest in memorials. Working parties of volunteers also spend Sunday afternoons clearing undergrowth and cleaning headstones.

Case Study: The Albert Memorial

Albert, Prince Consort to Queen Victoria, died from typhoid in 1861. One month after his death William Cubitt, Lord Mayor of London, called a public meeting to invite contributions for 'a monumental and national memorial'. A committee, helped by the Queen, invited nine architects to submit designs. There was a dispute about the form the memorial should take. Henry Cole of the South Kensington Museum called for a memorial college or hall. But the Queen preferred a monument 'in the common sense'.

Eventually they chose the design submitted by George Gilbert Scott. Scott claimed to have been inspired in his design by the thirteenth century 'Eleanor Crosses' erected by King Edward I to mark the place where Queen Eleanor's body rested

RIGHT: Angel after restoration.

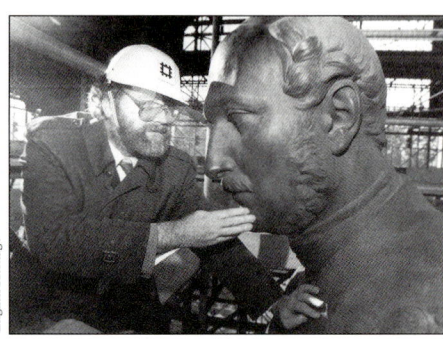

Inspecting Albert's head.

The Albert Memorial in Kensington Gardens, London.

on its way to London; and that the design of the canopy structure above the statue had been drawn from the character of a vast shrine or tabernacle, enriched with precious materials, evoking the ciboria above the altar in ancient basilicas. A close parallel is the monument designed by Meickle Kemp for Sir Walter Scott and erected in Edinburgh in the 1840s.

The memorial is a masterpiece of the Gothic Revival and stands over 55 metres high. The centrepiece of the monument is an outsize seated bronze statue of Prince Albert. He is depicted holding the catalogue of the Great Exhibition of 1851. High above the bronze figure of Prince Albert is a richly carved and gilded canopy of stone and bronze supported by granite columns with gables and filled with mosaics and with gilded pinnacles at the corners. Above the canopy rises a richly decorated, gilded flèche, faced in lead and constructed on an ironwork core.

A major feature of the memorial are the groups of statues and other carved figures at every level: two sets of four angels just below the cross and orb at the very top of the memorial; the four Christian and the four moral Virtues; high up on the memorial set in the niches of the flèche; eight figures of the

Sciences; Astronomy, Chemistry, Geology, Geometry, Rhetoric, Medicine; Philosophy and Physiology, on pedestals adjacent to the granite columns supporting the canopy; four groups representing the industrial arts and skills: Engineering, Agriculture, Commerce and Manufacture located just above the podium frieze; four of the continents: Europe, Asia, Africa and America, located at the extreme corners of the podium, and the great podium frieze of 169 figures, representing the world's artistic geniuses. The memorial was finally completed in 1876. The cost was about £150,000. Today the memorial poses a massive conservation challenge. A full survey carried out in 1985 showed significant corrosion between the ironwork core and leadwork cladding to the fleche. The entire memorial was covered in scaffolding in 1988. English Heritage was given responsibility for the repair and restoration of the monument in the summer of 1994, and in October 1994 had began a major scheme of repair and restoration which is expected to cost £14 million.

NEW MEMORIALS

From time to time the newspapers report on disputes about new memorials. Relatives appealed to a consistory court of the Church of England when a Lancashire vicar

English Heritage

Memorial plaques in rose garden at Hendon Crematorium.

would not allow them to put 'Dad' on a headstone and there were many letters and cartoons in the newspapers supporting them.

In the Lake District, admirers of Alfred Wainwright, author of the popular and detailed guides, have been frustrated in their efforts to have a large monument erected on the fells he climbed for over sixty years.

Pupils may like to give their views on which famous people alive today, or recently deceased, they think might qualify for a publicly-funded memorial and what form it should take.

DISPOSAL OF THE DEAD

Since 1901, cremation has been the most usual way of disposing of a dead body except for those belonging to faiths which insist on interment. Memorials for most of

us are little more than a name in a crematorium register, a small marker and a rose tree. Even this current practice is under discussion from 'green' campaigners who want to see the introduction of bio-degradable coffins and crematorium parks replaced by natural forests.

The Woodland Trust offer their own kind of memorial 'as a way of expressing sympathy to those who have lost a loved one or who wish to celebrate a birth or an anniversary. You can plant a single tree or a small stand of trees...or dedicate a grove of mature woodland. The dedication of an area of woodland is marked with a plaque within the grove or attached to a gate or stile in the wood boundary. Our woods also provide special places where ashes can be scattered in privacy.'

THE MILLENIUM

Discussions are underway at national and local levels about how to mark the end of the twentieth century and the start of the twenty-first. Some of the money raised by the National Lottery is to go towards projects, many in the form of buildings or permanent additions to the built environment. After studying memorials from the past, pupils may like to put forward proposals for the future.

Mike Corbishley

Memorial at Tadcaster to a police victim of IRA violence.

Case Study: A Jewish memorial in York

This newspaper cutting (below right) was one of several which recorded this new memorial to the massacre of the Jews in 1190. Attacks on Jews began in Autumn 1189 outside Westminster Abbey during the coronation of Richard, Coeur de Lion. Their entry to the abbey was barred and the Jews, identified by the yellow badges they were obliged to wear, lost their royal protection.

In the following Spring, hundreds of Jews who had lived in York for many generations were suddenly attacked by their neighbours. They sought refuge in the tower of the royal castle, Clifford's Tower. Over two days, 16 and 17 March 1190, hundreds of Jewish men, women and children were slaughtered.

Mike Corbishley

Memory of a tragedy

SOLDIERS from the Second Signal Regiment at York help school children plant 200,000 daffodils on the mound of the city's Clifford Tower in memory of hundreds of Jewish men, women and children slaughtered there by their fellow citizens in 1190. Directing operations, centre, is designer Gyora Novak, a Jewish artist.

The February Gold daffodil variety flowers in March, the month of the massacre, and its six petals shaped like a star recall the Star of David.

Funded to date by Americans, the bulb-planting project has the support of the monuments' agency English Heritage, which manages the Tower.

MEMORIALS ACROSS THE CURRICULUM

Studies of memorials can be part of many projects which meet National Curriculum requirements for students from 5 to 16.

HISTORY

Memorials are evidence about both individual lives and important events from prehistory to the present day. They can help pupils understand events and the lives of individuals in a chronological context. They raise questions as well as provide answers and in many cases, reasons for events, deaths and disaster are actually inscribed on the memorial stones. Memorials can be starting points for investigations and the writing of a narrative about the past. They can also send students to a range of additional

Memorial to Edith Cavell, St Martin's Place, London. She was executed in 1915 by the Germans for helping about 200 allied soldiers escape to neutral Holland.

historical sources in Record Offices and libraries and in books. Some exciting local history projects, based on memorials can introduce children to the lives of their family, famous men and women and notable local and national events (Key Stage 1) or illustrate either an aspect of the local community during a short

period of time or developments taught in the study units (Key Stage 2).

Memorial to a typographer, Birmingham.

ENGLISH

Memorials can promote reading, writing and speaking activities. They show how language, spelling and letter symbols have changed over time. Epitaphs and obituaries are models of specific styles of writing which pupils can be asked to imitate. Behind every memorial lies a story that can be retold as a narrative, poem or drama. The choice and location of memorials in the past and in the future are a subject for argument and debate.

ART

Local memorials can introduce pupils to knowledge and understanding of art at Key Stage 1,

■ in the locality

■ from past and present.

They are ideal sources for pupils to observe, record and develop as patterns, prints, photographs, collage and sculpture. They provide examples for studies of style in a social, historical and cultural context (Key Stage 3).

MATHS AND INFORMATION TECHNOLOGY

Data from graves and other memorials can be recorded in tables and graphs. Calculations can include average life spans at specific times in the past, differences in family size. Graves and memorials can be measured and sizes compared. Many shapes and patterns

can be seen on memorials and graves in a churchyard or cemetery can be classified according to age and condition. Data can be held on computer and analysed.

GEOGRAPHY

Memorials are identifying features of many localities, giving them not only a character but a map reference. Mapping skills can be developed in studies of plans of churchyards and cemeteries. Many inscriptions and epitaphs link the events of the people commemorated to a different part of the world. Some record place of birth as well as place of death providing information about changing settlement patterns and of developments in transport over time.

Gateway of India, Delhi. Built in 1927 to commemorate the visit of King George V and Queen Mary in 1911.

WORLD LINKS

You could extend the study of memorials in Britain to those around the world. You will find some examples of famous memorials in travel guides and books.

SCIENCE

Rock and stone used in memorials can be described and classified on the basis of their characteristics, including appearance, texture and permeability. Memorials, gravestones and cemeteries are habitats for living things including lichens and mini-beasts.

BIBLIOGRAPHY AND RESOURCES

Books for teachers

Churches and memorials

Bailey, B, **Churchyards of England and Wales**, Robert Hale, 1987, ISBN 1-85422-613-4.

Baker, M, **London Statues and Monuments**, Shire Publications, revised edition 1992, ISBN 0-7478-0162-2.

Brooks, C, **Mortal Remains: The History and Present State of the Victorian and Edwardian Cemeteries**, Wheaton, in association with the Victorian Society, 1989, ISBN 0-008-037098.

Burgess, F, **English Churchyard Memorials**, Lutterworth Press, 1963. The most authoritative book on churchyard memorials.

Child, M, **Discovering Churchyards**, Shire Publications, reprinted 1989, ISBN 0-85263-6.

Darke, Jo, **The Monument Guide to England and Wales: A National Portrait in Bronze and Stone**, Macdonald, 1991, ISBN 0-356-17609-6.

Goodman, A, **The Street Memorials of St Alban's Parish Church**, St Albans and Hertfordshire Architectural and Archaeology Society, 1987, ISBN 0-901194-08-5.

Jones, Jeremy, **How to Record Graveyards**, Council for British Archaeology and Rescue, 1984, ISBN 0-906780-43-8.

Jones, M, **The Dance of Death: Medallic art of the First World War**, British Museum Press, 1979, ISBN 0-7141-0846-4.

Leggett, J, **Local Heroines: A Womens History Gazetteer of England**, Scotland and Wales, Pandora Press, 1988, ISBN 0-86358-193-5.

Needham, A, **How to study an old church**, Batsford, 1944. Out of print but buy a copy if you see one. It is full of clear drawings.

Scott Anderson, A, **Roman Military Tombstones**, Shire Publications, 1984, ISBN 0-85263-571-0.

O'Neill, M, **West Sussex Literary, Musical and Artistic Links**, West Sussex Information Service, 1993, ISBN 0-86260-X.

Tilehurst, B, **The Titanic: Southampton's Memorials**, Waterfront Publications, Poole, reprinted 1992, ISBN 0-946184-30-5.

Walker, S, **Memorials to the Roman dead**, British Museum Press, 1985, ISBN 0-7141-1275-5.

Wilson, D, **The British Museum Book of Epitaphs,** British Museum Press, 1992, ISBN 0-7141-1726-9.

Teaching strategies

Barnicoat, J, **A Teacher's Guide to Newspapers and Conservation**, English Heritage, 1994, ISBN 1-85074-511-0.

Copeland, T, **A Teacher's Guide to Geography and the Historic Environment**, English Heritage, 1993, ISBN 1-85074-332-0.

Copeland, T, **A Teacher's Guide to Maths and the Historic Environment**, English Heritage, 1992, ISBN 1-85074-329-0.

Crispin, K, **A Teacher's Guide to Using Listed Buildings,** English Heritage, 1991, ISBN 1-85074-297-9.

Dix, B & Smart, R, **'Down among the deadmen', Archaeology in the town**, ed. Mike Corbishley, Archaeology for Schools series, Council for British Archaeology, 1982, ISSN 0262-897X.

Hill, JD with Mays, S, **Dead Men Don't Tell Tales?** A graveyard project for schools, Archaeology and Education Project, University of Southampton/Manpower Services Commission, 1987, ISBN 0-854-32282-5.

Moriarty, C, **'War memorials - a local study'**, Remnants No 14 Summer 1991, English Heritage.

Parvin, J, **Be Active: Science is Fun**, The Acid Test, Chemical Industry Education Centre, University of York, 1993, ISBN 1-85342-601-6. Contains activities for Key Stage 2 pupils on the effects of acid rain on lichens on gravestones.

Planel, P, **A Teacher's Guide to**

Battlefields, Defence, Conflict and Warfare, English Heritage, 1995, ISBN 1-85074-590-0.

Pownall, J, & Hudson, N, **A Teacher's Guide to Science and the Historic Environment**, English Heritage, 1992, ISBN 1-85074-331-2.

Books for children

Fewins, Clive, **Be a Church Detective: A Young Person's Guide to Old Churches**, The National Society and Church House Publishing, 1992, ISBN 0-7151-4790-0.

Patchett, T, **Johnny and the Dead**, Corgi Books, 1994, ISBN 0-552-52740-8. A humorous fantasy story about the reactions of some of the inhabitants of graves in a Victorian cemetery to the news that the council has decided to sell it to developers at a knock down price. For readers of twelve and above.

Pluckrose, Henry, **Local History Detective: Churches,** Simon and Schuster Education, 1993, ISBN 0-7501-0450-3.

Videos

God's Acre: Nature Conservation in the Churchyard, English Heritage, 1993, 24 minutes. Looks at various management techniques for the nature conservation of a churchyard.

In Memoriam: the archaeology of graveyards, English Heritage, 1990, 21 minutes. This video introduces and explores links between ecology, archaeology, art and social history and the evidence of local graveyards.

The Gripping Beast, Teknisk Film Compagni/English Heritage, 1957, 15 minutes. This animated film explores the various ways in which the gripping beast style of ornamentation was employed in Viking art and shows examples including jewellery and stone carving.

Contacts

For information about graveyard recording forms and the book, **How to record graveyards**, contact

Council for British Archaeology
Bowes Morrell House
111 Walmgate
York
YO1 2UA

Many Victorian cemeteries now have groups of local people interested in their preservation and conservation. Some have produced trails and guides and offer guided walks on special open days, for example,

The Friends of Kensal Green Cemetery, c/o The General Cemetery Company, Harrow Road, London W10 4RA.

The Undercliffe Cemetery Charity, Undercliffe Lane, Bradford, West Yorkshire BD3 0QD.

The Friends of Highgate Cemetery
5 View Road
Highgate
London N6 4DJ

The Imperial War Museum and the Royal Commission on the Historical Monuments of England is compiling an inventory of war memorials of all types from all periods. It is particularly keen to hear about school memorials.

The Research Officer,
National Inventory of War Memorials,
Imperial War Museum,
Lambeth Road,
London SE1 6HZ.

The Local Studies Department of Birmingham Library has an index to the inscriptions on tombs, gravestones and monuments from Birmingham and the surrounding counties transcribed by the Birmingham and Midland Society for Genealogy and Heraldry.

Acknowledgements

Thanks to Mrs Eileen Hall and Mrs Debbie England for allowing us to photograph some of their collections of memorial cups and other objects; Penguin Books and the translator, Oliver Bernard, for allowing us to publish the poem of Apollinaire; pupils and teachers at Great Oakley Primary School. The Friends of Highgate Cemetery.

Our Education Service aims to help teachers at all levels make better use of the resource of the historic environment. Educational groups can make free visits to over 400 historic properties cared for by English Heritage. The following booklets are free on request. **Free Educational Visits, Using the Historic Environment**. Our **Resources** catalogue is also available. Please contact:

**English Heritage
Education Service
429 Oxford Street
London
W1R 2HD**

**Tel: 0171 973 3442
Fax: 0171 973 3443**

OPPOSITE TOP: Eighteenth-century tombstone, Concord, New Hampshire, USA (Caneta Hankins).
OPPOSITE RIGHT: Confederate Army memorial, Atlanta, Georgia, USA (Mike Corbishley).
OPPOSITE LEFT: Cemetery at Ahwar, India with mausolea of maharajahs (Mike Corbishley).
OPPOSITE BOTTOM: Veterans' Day 11 November 1986, at the Vietnam Memorial in Washington, USA (Range/Bettmann/UPI Pictures).

GRAVE MEMORIAL RECORDING FORM

	CEMETERY or GRAVEYARD	KIRK DEIGHTON							
	DEDICATION or DENOMINATION	ALL SAINTS							
1	NAT. GRID REF.		S	E	3	9	9	5	0	5
2	DATE of RECORD			0	4	0	5	7	9
3	NAME of RECORDER or GROUP	M. JENKINSON							
4	MEMORIAL No. and LETTER				0	0	0	5	4
5	No. of COMPONENTS							0	1
6	ASSOCIATED FORM LETTERS								
7	Memorial type: 1. flat 2. head 3. tomb 4. foot 5. other								2
8	MATERIAL and GEOLOGY	SANDSTONE							
9	STONE MASON or UNDERTAKER								
10	Which faces are inscribed? — compass points				0	0	0	7
11	No. of people commemorated						0	0	2
12	TECHNIQUE of INSCRIPTION	INCISED							
13	Condition of monument: 1. sound, in situ 2. sound displaced 3 leaning or falling apart 4. collapsed 5. overgrown								1
14	Condition of inscription: 1. mint 2. clear but worn 3. mainly decipherable 4. traces 5. illegible or destroyed								2
15	DIMENSIONS (in mms.)	Height					1	3	9	7
16		Width					0	9	1	4
17		Thickness					0	0	9	2
18	PHOTOGRAPH NEGATIVE No.						0	0	3	3
19	ORIENTATION	which way stone faces							7